Sensational
6-Pointed Star Quilts
By Sara Nephew

Table of Contents
Introduction..2
2-Row Blocks..4-6
3-Row Blocks..7-14
Design Grids...15-16

The Quilts
Little Star..17

Showcase Quilts
#1 Native Star..18
#2 Oriental...20
#3 Blizzard...21
Twostep..22
All Nations Wall Hanging............................24
Rain Of Stars..33
Acapulco Sun...34
Blooming Garden...36
Symphony...38
Frogs And Lightning....................................40
Bunkhouse Blanket......................................42
Nova..44
Rosedance...46
Sparks..48

Quilts In Color...................................25-32
Cutting Directions....................................49
Index of Shapes..55

Dedication
Again, To my Husband, Dale Nephew

Credits
Unless expressly stated, all the quilts in this book were designed and pieced by Sara Nephew and machine quilted by Barbara Ford.
Special thanks to the pattern testers;
Annette Austin, Diane Coombs, Joan Dawson, Eda Haas, Jean Look-Krischano, Judy Rein, and Lessa Siegele. Their work is grearly appreciated.

Cover Graphics - Elizabeth Nephew
www.nephco.com
Photography....Carl Murray

©Sara Nephew 1999
All rights reserved. No part of this book may be copied or reproduced for commercial use without written permission from:
Clearview Triangle, 8311 180th St. S. E.,

Printed in the USA
Library of Congress Catalog Card Number: 99-94905
ISBN: 0-9621172-9-3

The correct finished quilt dimensions are given in the photo gallery on pg. 25-32

Introduction

The First Piece

There are two basic units to work with in this book. First, there is the pieced hexagonal block. Imagine these units as concentric hexagons. The first hexagon is formed by six triangles. The second hexagon is one row of triangles out on the graph paper, and the third hexagon is one more row out. (see diagram) On page 4 you will find an 11-page dictionary of 36 hexagonal blocks. These are 2- Row or 3-Row blocks. (Every 3-Row block has a 2-Row block inside of it.)

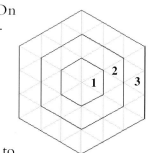

Perhaps you'd like to try designing a block. Keep in mind the basic shapes that can be cut (triangles, diamonds, teardrops, etc.) and begin on graph paper. Draw three concentric hexagons like the illustration. Using a soft color pencil or a marking pen, color the shapes you choose. Work from the center out, building a design. In each concentric row, decisions are made about repeat units, blank spaces, how to turn corners, etc. Each decision changes the design, so many different designs are possible.

The Second Piece

In a previous book, *Stars & Flowers: Three-Sided Patchwork*, I also worked with these hexagonal blocks. But in that book, the blocks were floated on the background using a plain (not pieced) setting triangle. Setting strips were also added, so each design floated on empty space. In this book, the second unit is the pieced setting triangle. Combining the pieced block with a pieced setting triangle is like combining two different square quilt blocks. Suddenly a new design is created where the two pieced sections meet. (All the designs in this book could be used with plain setting triangles, and many of the designs in *Stars & Flowers* could be used with pieced setting triangles.)

Below are drawings of pieced setting triangles. Some have been used in the quilts in this book, so you have instructions for constructing them. Many of the other triangles are easy to construct by looking at the shapes needed and turning to the cutting directions in the back of the book. Of course, not all the possibilities have been given. For a start, try reversing the values on them.

Symmetrical pieced triangles tend to be more useful than others in creating designs. Two of these are used in design grids on pg. 15 and 16 for you to copy and color. Be aware that though the design may be constructed originally of hexagons and triangles, it may be better to piece the design some other way.

About Borders

In this book the combination of the two pieced units produces repeat designs that are so strong, interesting and varied that I felt I had to choose a relatively narrow, plain border, the minimum frame for the quilt. Three quilts are an exception to this, the three **Showcase Quilts**. Each Showcase Quilt could begin with a block of your choice. Then six star points of your choice could be added. Three of the author's results are given, each a different star, each with a special border. The right border complements the center star, and repeats elements of its design, finishing it with a perfect frame.

If you decide to create your own star design using this method, you may wish to also create a special border for it, rather than use one of the pieced borders given. Draw the border design on graph paper and lay it along the edge of the star on the colored quilt diagram - or hold it up in the air at a distance from the pieced center star to get a feel for how well they go together. Do a little measuring and add setting strips of fabric to the center star to bring it up to the border size.

Graded Shading

Graded shading is a special effect that adds motion and interest to any quilt. It brings out first one element of a design and then another, circles here and triangles there, causing the quilt to sparkle. One area of the quilt is very light. Then as you move to another area the quilt darkens, gradually becoming very dark.

An easy way to achieve graded shading is to construct pieced blocks (and setting triangles) of different values. Make some blocks that are very light. Make some blocks that are very dark. Make some blocks that are high contrast (very light and dark within one block). Make some blocks of medium value with lots of color (jewel tones). You may want to play with fabric choices while you do this (a scrappy approach is fun here). Then lay them out from light to dark on a wall or floor to see what still needs to be constructed. Remember, each block or setting triangle must have dark and light in it to show the pattern. In a light block, the dark is much lighter. In a dark block, the light is much darker.

Choosing Values As Well As Colors

In order to use graded shading, the quilter must have some knowledge of value, one of the elements of design. Value, the lightness or darkness of a color (shading), is a tool that is used to achieve art effects and 3-D illusions. (See the book *Building Block Quilts*.) Like riding a bicycle, seeing color as value is a skill that can be learned, and once learned is never really forgotten.

There are favorite methods for judging the value of a fabric. Looking through a piece of colored plastic (usually red) is one technique, and another approach sometimes mentioned is viewing a design through the wrong end of a pair of binoculars. Some quilters get extra use from their glasses by removing them. A red sheet of plastic can help you judge values, but does not work well with some colors. Reds, yellows, and oranges are different from other hues. These colors glow to our eyes and this glow makes them lighter in value. So the warm tones can be hard to judge when mixed in with other colors. But they add life and vibrancy to a quilt.

My favorite way to determine value is to squint. Narrowing the eyes so less light comes in reduces the color element and increases perception of value. Squinting also allows the comparison of the lightness or darkness of busy or larger prints. The eye mixes the light and dark parts of these prints when we see them from a distance, or in a reduced light. This allows us to compare them, and to judge.

Begin to compare fabrics by laying one over the other. Choose a fabric you can be sure of, perhaps a definite light. Lay it out flat and put another fabric against it. Then lay it over the other fabric. Are they both light? Is one lighter than the other? When you have as many light fabrics as needed, begin to choose definite darks next. Last of all, choose mediums. Lay a medium fabric across the light fabric and then across the dark fabric. Try to find a medium that is exactly in between the light and the dark value, for a complete value range.

For best results, work with fewer layers of material, as thick folds may cast a shadow and fool the eye. Also avoid a lighter selvage or torn edge, folding distracting elements under.

When designs emphasize value, often the weaknesses of a quilter's fabric collection begin to show up. Some quilters, without knowing it, have concentrated on medium colors without collecting any light or dark fabrics. Others have all light and dark, with few mediums. This may require some purchases to supply the missing range of colors. Future quilts will gain added radiance both from an expanded fabric library and from the knowledge acquired by working with value in your quilts.

A final note: the quilt patterns in this book are arranged with the easiest at the beginning and the more challenging at the end.

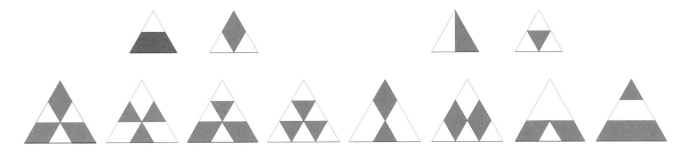

2-ROW BLOCKS   3" triangle size

Twinkle

Cut for one block:

1	light	7½"	triangle
3	light	3"	triangle
6	dark	2¾"	diamond

Sew two diamonds and a dark 3" triangle into a strip as shown. Make two more of these. Sew these strips onto the triangle to make a hexagon.

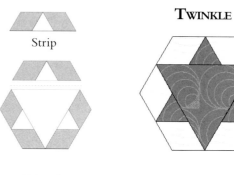

Star Bright

Cut for one block:

1	dark	5"	hexagon
6	light	3"	triangle
6	dark	2¾"	diamond

Sew three triangles to three separate sides of the hexagon to make the center triangle. Continue as in **Twinkle** above.

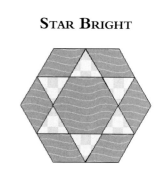

Spinner

Sandwich-piece six half-diamonds from a 1⅞" set of light and dark strips. Then cut for one block:

6	light	3"	triangle
6	dark	3"	triangle

Sew a light and a dark triangle onto a half-diamond to make a wedge as shown. Make five more of these. Sew the wedges into two groups of three, pressing the two seams as shown. Then sew these two half-hexes together, matching the center points and pinning.

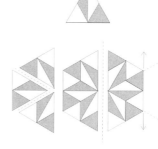
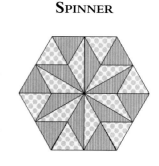

Traditional

Cut for one block:

6	light	2¾"	diamond
12	dark	3"	triangle

Make six wedges and assemble three and three like **Spinner**.

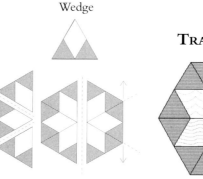

2-ROW BLOCKS 3" triangle size

Star Surrounded

Cut for one block:

1	light	7½"	triangle
3	light	3"	triangle

Sandwich-piece six half-diamonds from a 1⅞" set of strips. Sew two half-diamonds and a light 3" triangle into a strip as shown. Make two more of these. Sew these strips onto the triangle to make a hexagon. (Reversing the light and dark values gives a new look to the design.)

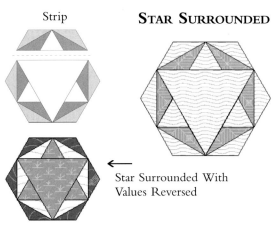

← Star Surrounded With Values Reversed

Wood Rose

Cut for one block:

1	dark	5"	hexagon
6	light	3"	triangle

Sew three triangles to three separate sides of the hexagon to make the center triangle. Continue as in **Star Surrounded** above. (Reversing the light and dark values gives a new look to the design.)

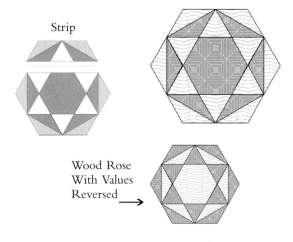

Wood Rose With Values Reversed →

Morning Glory

1. Cut six light 3" triangles. Sandwich-piece six half-triangles from a 2" set of light and dark strips.

2. Sandwich-piece six half-diamonds from a 1⅞" set of strips. Sew the half-triangles three and three to make the center of the flower (twirl). Sew three light 3" triangles onto the center hexagon to make a larger triangle. Sew two half-diamonds and a light 3" triangle into a strip as shown. Make two more of these. Sew these strips onto the center triangle to make a hexagon.

Twirl   Center Triangle

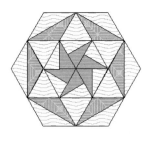

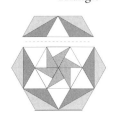

Rose Star

Cut for one block:

1	dark	7½"	triangle
3	dark	3"	triangle
6	dark	3⅜"	teardrop
12	light	3½"	triangle half (6 left/6 right)

From the teardrops and the triangle halves, piece six teardrop units as shown. Sew two teardrop units and a dark 3" triangle into a strip. Make two more of these. Sew these strips onto the triangle to make a hexagon.

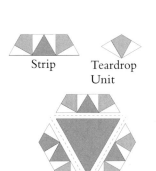

Strip   Teardrop Unit

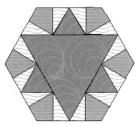

2-ROW BLOCKS 3" triangle size

Sunflower
Cut for one block:

1	dark	5"	hexagon
6	light	3"	triangle
6	light	3⅜"	teardrop
12	dark	3½"	triangle half (6 left/6 right)

Sew three triangles to the hexagon to make a larger triangle. Piece six teardrop units as shown. Sew two teardrop units and a light 3" triangle into a strip as shown. Make two more of these. Sew these strips onto the larger triangle to make a hexagon again.

Teardrop Unit

Strip

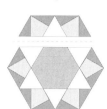

SUNFLOWER

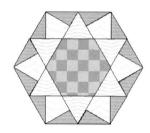

Rock Candy
Piece as for **Sunflower**, but use a 7½" light triangle in the center.

Crystalline
Piece as for **Sunflower**, but Sandwich-piece six half-triangles from a 2" set of light and dark strips. Sew three and three to make a twirl in the center.

ROCK CANDY

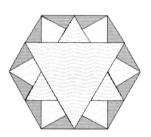

CRYSTALLINE

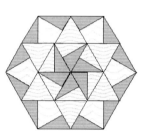

Pinwheel
Cut for one block:

1	dark	5"	hexagon
6	light	2¾"	diamond

Sandwich piece six half-triangles from a 2" set of strips. Sew three half-triangles to the hexagon to make a triangle as shown. Sew two diamonds and a half-triangle into a strip as shown. Make two more of these. Sew these strips onto the center triangle to make a hexagon again.

PINWHEEL

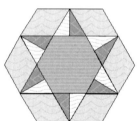

Flaming Pinwheel
Sandwich-piece six half-triangles from a 2" set of light and dark strips. Sew three and three as shown and use as the center of the **Pinwheel** block.

Twirl

FLAMING PINWHEEL

Center Triangle

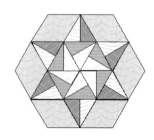

6

3-ROW BLOCKS 3" triangle size

Headlight

1. Cut for one block:

1	dark	7½"	triangle
6	dark	3"	triangle
6	light	3"	triangle
6	light	2¾"	diamond
6	dark	5¼"	flat pyramid from 2¾" strip

2. Assemble one **Twinkle** block, pg. 4. Using two dark 3" triangles and one light 3" triangle make a flat pyramid shape as shown. Make two more of these. Sew three of these flat pyramid shapes onto three separate sides of the **Twinkle** block to make a larger triangle.

3. Sew one light 3" triangle and two dark flat pyramids into a strip as shown. Make two more of these. Sew this strip onto each side of the larger triangle to make a hexagon again.

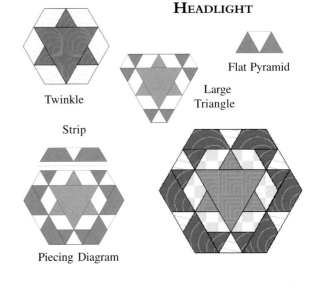

HEADLIGHT

Ribbon Wrap

1. Cut for one block:

1	light	7½"	triangle
9	light	3"	triangle
6	dark	2¾"	diamond
6	light	2¾"	diamond

2. Assemble one **Twinkle** block, pg. 4. Sandwich-piece six **left** and six **right** half-triangles from 2" light and dark strips. Using the left and right half-triangles and one light triangle make a flat pyramid shape as shown. Make five more of these. Sew three of these flat pyramid shapes onto three separate sides of the **Twinkle** block to make a larger triangle.

3. Sew two light diamonds and a flat pyramid shape into a strip as shown. Make two more of these. Sew this strip onto each side of the larger triangle to make a hexagon again.

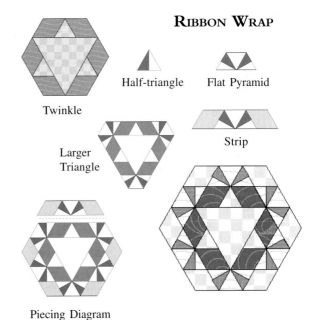

RIBBON WRAP

Twist Tie

1. Cut for one block:

12	dark	3"	triangle
6	light	2¾"	diamond
6	light	7½"	flat pyramid from 2¾" strip

2. From one light 2¾" diamond, two dark 3" triangles, and one light 7½" flat pyramid, assemble a wedge as shown. Make six of these. Sew three and three and sew across the middle to make a hexagon block.

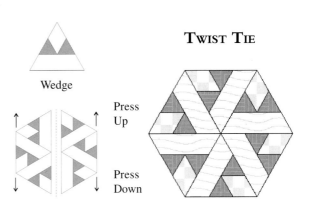

TWIST TIE

7

3-ROW BLOCKS   3" triangle size

Blooming Star

1. Cut for one block:

1	dark	5"	hexagon
6	light	3"	triangle
6	light	2¾"	diamond
6	dark	5¼"	flat pyramid from 2¾" strip
3	dark	5"	long diamond from 2¾" strip

2. Sew three light 3" triangles onto the hexagon to make a large center triangle. Sew a long diamond, a flat pyramid, and a 3" triangle together to make Unit A according to the diagram. Make three of these. Sew onto the center triangle to make a larger triangle. Sew two light diamonds and a dark flat pyramid into a strip as shown. Make two more of these. Sew this strip onto each side of the larger triangle to make a hexagon block.

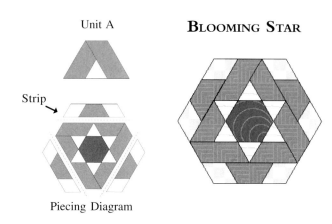

Cut Paper Star

1. Cut for one block:

1	light	5"	hexagon
12	dark	3"	triangle
6	light	3"	triangle
6	light	2¾"	diamond
6	dark	3⅜"	teardrop
12	light	3½"	triangle half (6 left/6 right)

2. Assemble one **Sunflower** block, pg. 6. Sandwich-piece 12 half-triangles. From two half-triangles and one dark triangle, make a flat pyramid shape as shown. Make five more of these. Sew three of these flat pyramid shapes onto three separate sides of the **Sunflower** block to make a larger triangle.

3. Sew two light diamonds and a flat pyramid shape into a strip as shown. Make two more of these. Sew this strip onto each side of the larger triangle to make a hexagon again.

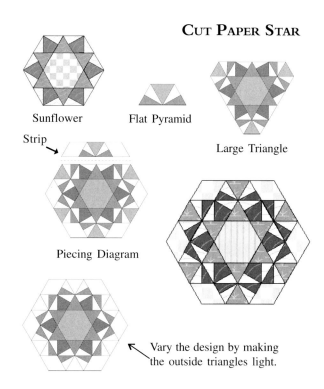

Rose

1. Cut for one block:

1	dark	5"	hexagon
6	light	3"	triangle
6	light	5¼"	flat pyramid from 2¾" strip
12	both	1⅞"	half-diamond

2. Assemble one **Wood Rose** block as shown on pg. 5. Sew light 5¼" flat pyramids on three separate sides of the **Wood Rose** block to make a larger triangle. Sew two half-diamonds and a light flat pyramid into a strip as shown. Make three of these. Sew this strip on three sides of the larger triangle to make a hexagon again.

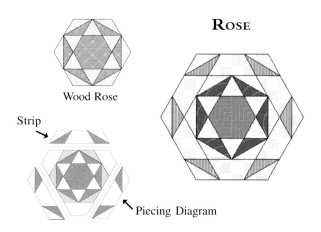

3-ROW BLOCKS 3" triangle size

Crowned Star

1. Cut for one block:

1	light	7½"	triangle
15	light	3"	triangle
6	dark	3"	triangle
6	dark	2¾"	diamond
6	both	1⅞"	half-diamond

2. Make one block of **Star Surrounded** according to the directions on pg. 5.

3. Using two light and one dark 3" triangles, make a pieced flat pyramid as shown. Sew it onto three separate sides of the **Star Surrounded** block to make a larger triangle.

4. Using two light 3" triangles, one 3" dark triangle, and two dark diamonds, make a strip as shown. Make two more of these. Sew this strip onto three sides of the larger triangle to make a hexagon again.

CROWNED STAR

Flat Pyramid

Larger Triangle

Strip
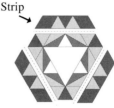
Piecing Diagram

North Star

1. Cut for one block:

1	dark	5"	hexagon
6	light	3"	triangle
6	light	5¼"	flat pyramid from 2¾" strip
12	dark	2¾"	diamond

2. Assemble one **Star Bright** block as shown on pg. 4. Sew three light flat pyramids onto three separate sides of the **Star Bright** block to make a larger triangle. Sew two diamonds and a flat pyramid into a strip as shown. Make two more of these. Sew this strip onto each side of the larger triangle to make a hexagon again.

NORTH STAR

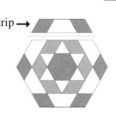
Star Bright
Larger Triangle

Strip →
Piecing Diagram
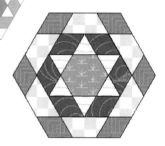

Sheriff's Star

Assemble one **Twinkle** block as shown on pg. 4. Continue to assemble as in **North Star** block.

SHERIFF'S STAR

Twinkle

Facets

Use a flat pyramid shape made from two light 3" triangles and one dark 3" triangle in the final strip. Sew onto three sides of the North Star block.

FACETS

Flat Pyramid

Strip

9

3-ROW BLOCKS   3" triangle size

Floating Crystal

1. Cut for one block:

1	light	7½"	triangle
3	light	3"	triangle
6	dark	3⅜"	teardrop
12	light	3½"	triangle half (6 left/6 right)
6	light	5¼"	flat pyramid from 2¾" strip

2. Assemble one **Rock Candy** block, pg. 6. Then sew three flat pyramids onto three separate sides of the **Rock Candy** block to make a larger triangle. Sew two teardrop units and a flat pyramid into a strip as shown. Make two more of these. Sew this strip onto each side of the larger triangle to make a hexagon again.

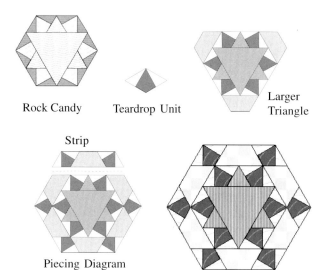

Mariner's Star and Radiant Star

Instead of cutting light flat pyramids, construct a flat pyramid from two dark and one light 3" triangles (Mariner's Star) or two light and one dark 3" triangles (Radiant Star). Continue to piece as in **Floating Crystal** above. This is an example of how a small change in piecing or coloring can make a large change in the appearance of a block.

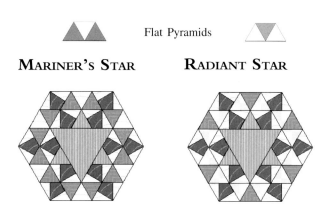

Diamond Star

1. Cut for one block:

1	dark	7½"	triangle
9	dark	3"	triangle
12	light	3"	triangle

2. Assemble one block of **Star Surrounded**, as on pg. 5, but position the light side of the half-diamonds to the center. Then from two light 3" triangles and one dark 3" triangle make a flat pyramid shape as shown. Make five more of these. Sew three of these flat pyramid shapes onto three separate sides of the **Star Surrounded** block to make a larger triangle.

3. Sew two half-diamonds and a flat pyramid shape into a strip as shown. Make two more of these. Sew this strip onto each side of the larger triangle to make a hexagon again.

3-ROW BLOCKS 3" triangle size

Floral Medallion *from a design by Willyne Daniel-Fenton*
1. Cut for one block:

1	dark	5"	hexagon
6	light	3"	triangle
6	dark	5¼"	flat pyramid from 2¾" strip
6	dark	3⅜"	teardrop
12	light	3½"	triangle half (6 left/6 right)

2. Assemble one **Wood Rose** block as shown on pg. 5. Sew three flat pyramids onto three separate sides of the **Wood Rose** block to make a larger triangle. Piece six teardrop units. Using two teardrop units and one flat pyramid make a strip as shown. Make two more of these. Sew this strip onto each side of the larger triangle to make a hexagon again.

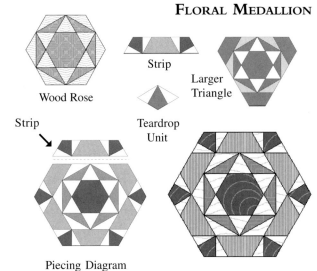

Chain
1. Cut for one block:

1	light	5"	hexagon
6	light	3"	triangle
12	dark	2¾"	diamond
6	light	5¼"	flat pyramid from 2¾" strip

2. From a light triangle, two dark diamonds, and a light flat pyramid, assemble a pieced flat pyramid according to the diagram. Make six of these. Sew one pieced flat pyramid to the light hexagon, leaving the left ½" of the seam unsewn.

3. Sew the remaining pieced flat pyramids on clockwise in order according to the diagram. Then finish sewing the first seam from #2 above.

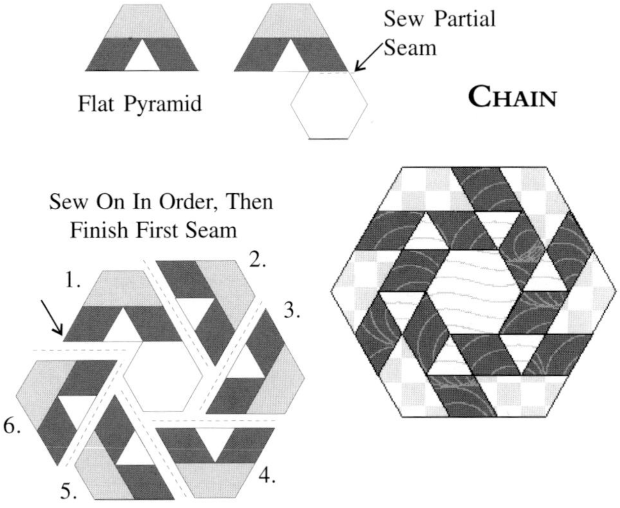

Wings
1. Cut for one block:

1	light	7½"	triangle
9	light	3"	triangle
6	dark	3"	triangle
6	light	2¾"	diamond
6	dark	5¼"	flat pyramid from 2¾" strip

2. Assemble Unit A as shown from two light 3" triangles and two dark 5¼" flat pyramids. Make three of these. Sew onto the 7½" light triangle to make a larger triangle.

3. Using two dark 3" triangles, one light 3" triangle, and two light diamonds, make a strip as shown. Make three of these. Sew this strip onto each side of the larger triangle to make a hexagon again.

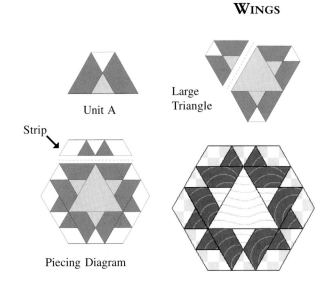

11

3-ROW BLOCKS   3" triangle size

Galaxy *from a design by Peggy Chandler*
1. Cut for one block:

1	dark	5"	hexagon
6	light	3"	triangle
24	both	3"	sandwich-pieced half-triangle
6	light	5¼"	flat pyramid from 2¾" strip

2. (The half-triangles should have the dark on the left.) Sew three half-triangles to three separate sides of the hexagon to make the center triangle.

3. Using two half-triangles, one light 3" triangle and one light flat pyramid, make a pieced hexagon as shown. Make five more of these.

4. Using two pieced hexagons and two half-triangles, make a long hex as shown. Make two more of these. Sew the long hexes onto the central triangle in order according to the diagram, adding half-triangles to the long hex as shown on the diagram.

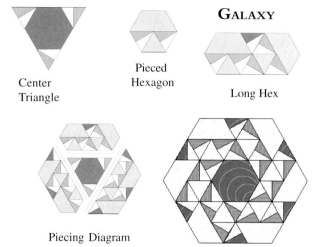

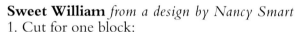

Sweet William *from a design by Nancy Smart*
1. Cut for one block:

6	both	1⅞"	sandwich-pieced half-diamond
18	dark	3"	triangle
12	light	2¾"	diamond

2. Using three dark triangles, two light diamonds, and half-diamond, make a pieced wedge. Make six of these.

3. Sew the pieced wedges together three and three, pressing the seams as shown. Sew the two halves together, matching the centers and pinning.

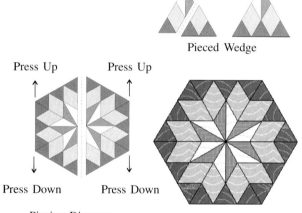

Framed Star
1. Cut for one block:

1	dark	5"	hexagon
6	light	3"	triangle
3	dark	5¼"	flat pyramids from 2¾" strip
3	dark	9¾"	flat pyramids from 2¾" strip

2. Assemble one **Star Surrounded** block as shown on pg. 5. Then sew the 5¼" dark flat pyramids to three separate sides of the **Star Surrounded** block to make a larger triangle shape. Sew the 9¾" flat pyramids onto the larger triangle to make a hexagon again.

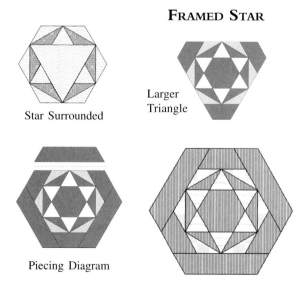

3-ROW BLOCKS   3" triangle size

Mill Wheel *from a design by Mona Wadington*
1. Cut for one block:

1	dark	5"	hexagon
6	dark	3"	triangle
6	dark	2¾"	diamond
6	light	5¼"	flat pyramid from 2¾" strip
6	both	3"	sandwich-pieced matching triangle

2. Using a dark triangle, a dark diamond, a matching triangle pair, and a light flat pyramid, assemble a pieced flat pyramid according to the diagram. Make six of these. Sew one pieced flat pyramid to the dark hexagon, leaving the right ½" of the seam unsewn.

3. Sew the remaining pieced flat pyramids on counterclockwise in order according to the diagram. Then finish sewing the first seam from #2 above.

Flat Pyramid

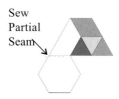
Sew Partial Seam

MILL WHEEL

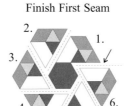
Sew On In Order, Then Finish First Seam
Piecing Diagram

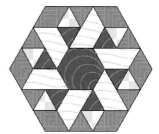

Kings and Queens
1. Cut for one block:

1	dark	7½"	triangle
9	dark	3"	triangle
12	light	2¾"	diamond
12	both	3"	sandwich-pieceed half-triangle

2. Assemble one **Twinkle** block with values reversed according to the directions on pg. 4. Sew two half-triangles and a dark 3" triangle into a pieced flat pyramid as shown. Make six of these. Sew three pieced flat pyramids onto the **Twinkle** block as shown to make a larger triangle.

3. Add two light diamonds to the remaining flat pyramid shapes to make a strip as shown. Make three of these. Sew this strip onto each side of the larger triangle to make a hexagon again.

Twinkle Reversed

KINGS AND QUEENS

Flat Pyramid

Larger Triangle

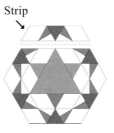
Strip
Piecing Diagram

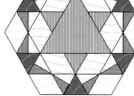

Setting In A Teardrop
1. Right sides together, sew a teardrop unit to one inside edge of a seamed pair of diamonds or half-diamonds. Sew only up to the seam allowance and backstitch. Remove from under pressor foot.

2. Line up the two remaining raw edges. Begin at the inside seam allowance, take a backstitch and seam to the outside edge.

Stop and Backstitch   Backstitch Again
  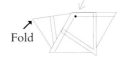
1.   2.
                       Fold

13

3-ROW BLOCKS   3" triangle size

Bouquet

1. Cut for one block:

3	dark	3"	triangle
12	light	3"	triangle
3	light	2¾"	diamond
12	dark	2¾"	diamond
6	dark	3⅜"	teardrop
12	light	3½"	triangle half

2. Assemble the dark triangles and the light diamonds according to the diagram to make the center triangle.

3. Piece six teardrop units as shown. Sew two dark diamonds together, starting with a backstitch at the inside seam allowance and stitching to the outside edge. Set one teardrop unit into each pair of dark diamonds as shown to make the flower. *(See pg. 13.)*

4. Assemble two light triangles and two flowers into a pieced strip as shown. Make three of these. Sew the strips onto the center triangle in order, adding light triangles to the strips according to the diagram at right.

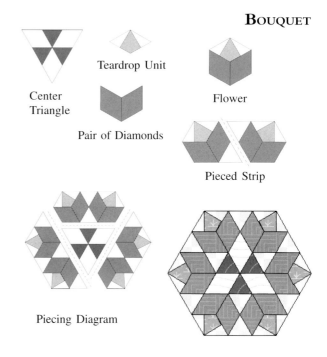

Circus *from a design by Yvonne Phenicie*

1. Cut for one block:

1	dark	4⅛"	triangle
3	dark	1⅞"	triangle
6	light	1⅜"	diamond
12	light	3"	triangle
6	dark	3"	triangle
6	dark	2¾"	diamond
6	light	5¼"	flat pyramid from 2¾" strip

2. Sew two light 1⅜" diamonds and a dark 1⅞" triangle into a strip as shown. Make three of these. Sew these strips onto the 4⅛" triangle to make a small pieced star.

3. Make a **Star Bright** block, pg. 4., using the small pieced star from #2 above as the center hex.

4. Sew one dark and two light 3" triangles into a flat pyramid shape as shown. Make three of these. Sew these flat pyramid shapes onto three separate sides of the Twinkle block to make a larger triangle.

5. Sew two flat pyramids and a 3" dark triangle into a strip as shown. Make three of these. Sew this strip onto each side of the larger triangle to make a hexagon block.

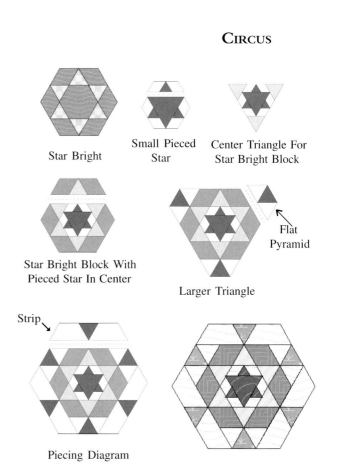

14

DESIGN GRID - Copy This Page And Color In Your Choice Of Blocks

15

DESIGN GRID – Copy This Page And Color In Your Choice Of Blocks

LITTLE STAR

3" triangle size
Quilt without borders: 28" x 31¾"

All fabric 42" wide prewashed.
Fabric Requirements:
¾ yds. star fabric
½ yds. star background fabric
½ yds. setting triangle fabric
½ yds. border fabric

Directions:
1. Cut for one Little Star:

1	dark	4⅛"	triangle
3	dark	1⅞"	triangle
6	light	1⅝"	diamond

Assemble according to the diagram. Make 23 of these.

Piecing Diagram

LITTLE STAR

2. Cut 44 light 3" setting triangles. Sew triangles on opposite sides of 17 Little Stars as shown to make diamond-shaped blocks.

3. For each partial block:

1	Little Star
1	3" light setting triangle
2	triangle halves from 3" triangle (1 left/1 right)

Assemble according to the diagram. You will need six of these.

4. Cut for each fill-in piece:

1	3" setting triangle
2	2¾" x 3⅜" quarter hex (1 left/1 right)

Assemble according to the diagram at left. You will need four of these.

5. Assemble the quilt top in five rows. Rows 1, 3, and 5 have a partial block top and bottom. Rows 2 and 4 have a fill-in piece top and bottom. Add a final 3" outer border to complete the Little Star quilt.

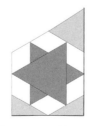

PARTIAL BLOCK

FILL-IN PIECE

SHOWCASE QUILT #1 - NATIVE STAR

Piece any 3-row block at the 3" triangle size. Then make this quilt to frame it. Annette Austin used the Wings block, pg. 11.

3" triangle size
Quilt with pieced border:
47¼" x 50½"

All fabric 42" wide prewashed.
Fabric Requirements:
1½ yds. dark fabric
2 yds. light fabric

Note: This design looks best with a block that has a star in the middle. If you are using a block with a center hexagon, use a color for the hexagon that completes the center star.

Directions:
1. Cut for one setting triangle:

3	light	3"	triangle
2	dark	2¾"	diamond
1	light	2¾"	diamond

Use one dark diamond and two light triangles to make a pieced triangle as shown. Use a dark diamond, a light diamond, and a light triangle to make a pieced strip. Sew the pieced triangle and the pieced strip together as shown. Make six of these.

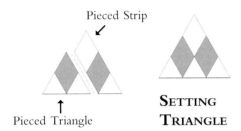

Pieced Strip
Pieced Triangle
SETTING TRIANGLE

2. Cut for fill-in pieces:

4	background triangle half (from 8" triangle)
4	background 7¼" x 12½" rectangle trimmed★

★Place two rectangles right sides together and trim one end to a 60° angle as shown. You will get one and one reverse. Make two of each.

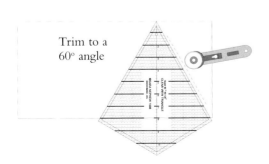

Trim to a 60° angle

3. Assemble the quilt top as shown in the piecing diagram. Add a 2¼" inner border of light fabric. Trim left and right edges even as necessary.

To piece the Native Star Border:
4. Cut for one section:

2	dark	2¾"	diamond
1	light	3"	triangle
1	light	3½"	triangle half ★
1	light	5¾"	triangle half ★
1	light	8"	triangle half ★

★Cut from a triangle this size. Use the other triangle half for the other border section.

Assemble a Native Star border section as shown. Make eight of these. Make eight reverse. Sew two sections and two reverse sections together alternately into a border panel. Make four border panels. Sew panels to the top and bottom of the quilt top. Cut four 5¾" x 7½" rectangles of light fabric and add to both ends of each remaining border panel. Sew these long borders to left and right. Add a final 4½" outer border to complete the quilt.

Border Section   Reverse Border Section

18

SHOWCASE QUILT #1 - NATIVE STAR

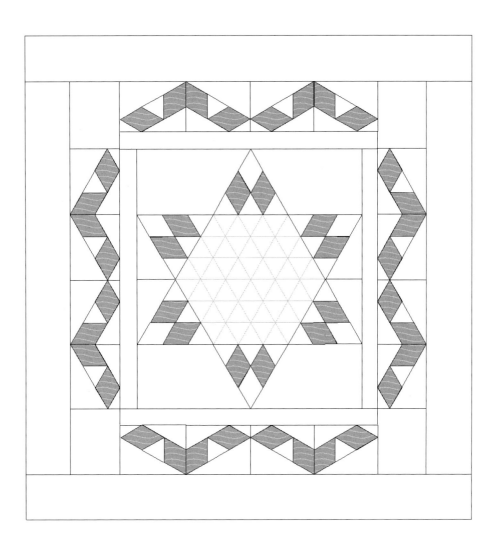

Piecing Diagram

SHOWCASE QUILT #2 - ORIENTAL

Piece any 3-row block at the 3" triangle size. Then make this quilt to frame it. Sara used Sweet William, pg.12, and jewel tone plaids.

3" triangle size
Quilt with borders: 40" x 44"

All fabric 42" wide prewashed.
Fabric Requirements:
1½ yds. dark fabric
2 yds. light fabric

Directions:
1. Cut for one setting triangle:

1	dark	3"	triangle
3	light	3"	triangle
2	dark	1⅞"	diamond half
1	light	2¾"	diamond

Line up points of the large and small diamond halves as shown when seaming. Assemble setting triangle according to the diagram. Make six.

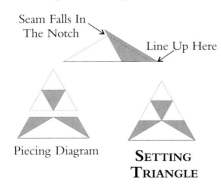

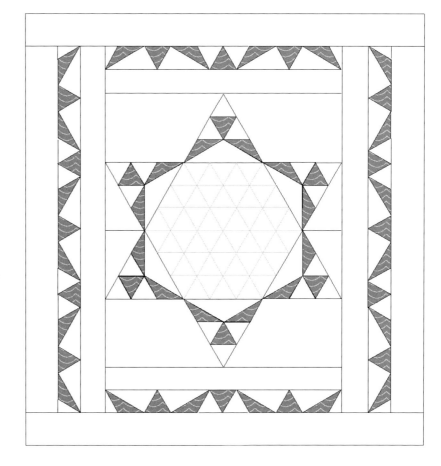

2. Assemble star section as for **Showcase Quilt#1**. Then add a 3" border strip at the top and bottom. (Adjust 3" width as necessary so center section length matches left and right pieced border length.)

To piece the Oriental border:
3. Cut:

6	dark	3"	triangle
12	light	3"	triangle
20	light	5¾"	triangle half ★
20	dark	1⅞"	diamond half
8	light	3½"	triangle half ★

★Cut from triangle. Make 10 large flat pyramids as shown. Make 6 small flat pyramids as shown.

4. Assemble the top and bottom Oriental borders as shown. (Finish all ends of pieced borders with a 3½" triangle half.)

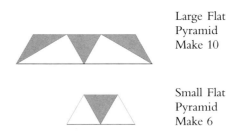

Large Flat Pyramid
Make 10

Small Flat Pyramid
Make 6

5. Sew on the top and bottom borders. Then add a 3" border strip at left and right. Assemble and sew on the left and right Oriental borders as shown. Add a final 4" border to complete the quilt.

SHOWCASE QUILT #3 - BLIZZARD

*Piece any 3-row block at the 3" triangle size. Then make this quilt to frame it. Sara used the **Headlight** block on pg. 7, reversing values.*

3" triangle size
Quilt with pieced borders: 42¼" x 45½"

All fabric 42" wide prewashed.
Fabric Requirements:
1½ yds. light fabric
2 yds. dark fabric

Directions:
1. Cut for one setting triangle:

3	dark	3" triangle
3	both	3" matching triangle
		(sandwich-pieced)

Assemble setting triangle as shown. Make six of these.

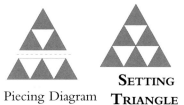

Piecing Diagram   **SETTING TRIANGLE**

2. Cut fill-in pieces and assemble star section as for Showcase Quilt #1. Add a 2¾" inner border of background fabric.

To piece the Blizzard border:
3. Cut:

4	light	3"	triangle
44	both	3"	matching triangle (sandwich-pieced)
8	dark		quarter hexes from a 2¾" x 3⅜" rectangle (4 left/4 right)
20	dark	5¼"	flat pyramid (2¾" strip)
8	dark	3½"	triangle half from triangle (4 left/4 right)

Divide these pieces into four sets and assemble four border sections as shown. Sew a border section on left and right. Cut four dark 3⅝" x 5" rectangles. (Measure the width of the top and adjust the 3⅝" measurement. Or match centers, sew on pieced border, and trim off excess.) Sew this dark rectangle on each end of both remaining borders. Sew these borders on top and bottom. Add a final 3" border to complete the quilt.

21

TWOSTEP

3" triangle size
Quilt with borders: 78" x 89¼"

All fabric 42" wide prewashed.
Fabric requirements:
1¼ yds. each tan/white fabric for stripped triangles (2¼ yds. if sandwich piecing as in #1)
2 yds. star fabric
½ yd. star background fabric
¾ yd. large diamonds fabric
1½ yds. border fabric

Directions:
1. Cut for each stripped triangle:

1	light	3"	triangle
1	dark	5¼"	flat pyramid from 2¾" strip

Sew together as shown to make a stripped triangle. You will need 128 for Twostep. OR: Sew 3" strips of white and tan fabric together lengthwise. Cut 5½" triangles from each side of this set of strips. Use the triangles with the dark tip in **Rosedance**. Trim ¼" from the bottom of each triangle.

2. Make 23 Twinkle blocks with values reversed, according to the directions on pg. 4. Sew a light-tipped stripped triangle on three separate sides of each Twinkle block to make the triangular Twostep block as shown at right.

3. Cut three 5" diamonds for each alternate block. Assemble with three stripped triangles into the alternate block as shown. Make 22 Alternate Blocks.

4. For each Twostep partial block cut:

1	star	triangle half cut from an 8" triangle
1	star	triangle half cut from a 3½" triangle
1	star	3" triangle
3	light	2¾" background diamond

Add two stripped triangles and assemble as shown for a left or right partial Twostep block. Trim the stripped triangle even with the other pieces as shown (or wait till the top is together and trim then). Make two of each.

5. For each alternate finishing piece cut:

| 1 | 5" | diamond |
| 1 | diamond half from a 3⅛" strip |

Add two stripped triangles and assemble as shown. Make three left and three right fill-in pieces.

6. Assemble the blocks and Alternate Blocks into five vertical rows, as shown in the quilt diagram. Add a final 5½" border to complete the quilt.

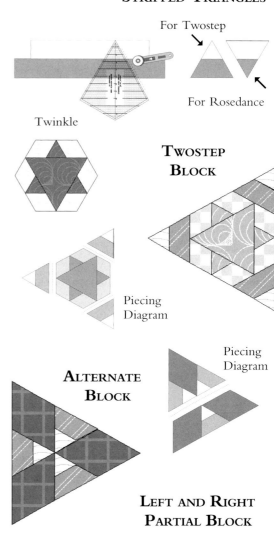

STRIPPED TRIANGLES

For Twostep

For Rosedance

Twinkle

TWOSTEP BLOCK

Piecing Diagram

ALTERNATE BLOCK

Piecing Diagram

LEFT AND RIGHT PARTIAL BLOCK

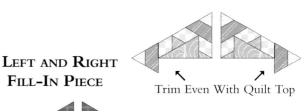

LEFT AND RIGHT FILL-IN PIECE

Trim Even With Quilt Top

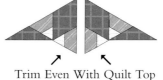

Trim Even With Quilt Top

TWOSTEP

ALL NATIONS WALL HANGING

> 3" triangle size
> Quilt without borders: 27½" x 32"

Note: vary blocks as desired. You may wish to lay everything out on a design wall before assembling the individual blocks.

Directions:

1. Piece these 2-row blocks:
   - 3 Twinkle, pg. 4
   - 3 Star Surrounded, pg. 5

2. Cut for each setting triangle:

2	light	3"	triangle
1	dark	2¾"	diamond

Assemble according to the diagram.

SETTING TRIANGLE

All fabric 42" wide prewashed.
Fabric Requirements:
Start with six 7½" selvage-to-selvage strips; two light, two medium, two dark colors. Add scraps for variety as desired.
½ yd. background fabric

3. Sew a setting triangle on three separate sides of each 2-row block. Make six of these block triangles. Sew into two sets of three and sew together across the center.

4. Cut a 14½" triangle of background fabric and bisect this to produce two half-triangles. Sew these as shown to top left and top right to complete the wall hanging.

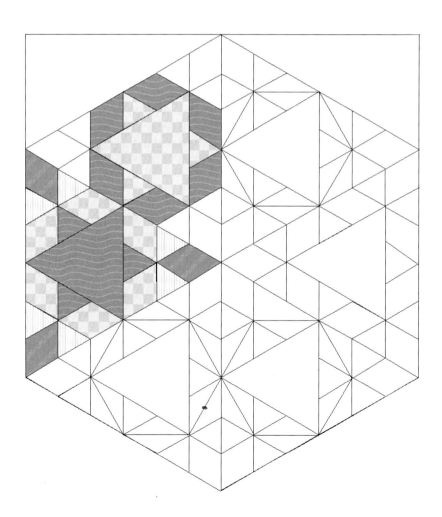

Symphony; 63½" x 79". The author's daughter Elizabeth and her fiancé Avrum Cohen requested a chupah (wedding canopy) for their Jewish wedding. What a privilege to make an heirloom like this! Blue and white, graded from light at the top to dark at the bottom, was their request. This quilt is the result. Circular patterns sparkle and shimmer like moonlight reflecting off of water.

Acapulco Sun; 43½" x 65". Jean was inspired by the pattern name to produce a golden, glowing quilt. She worked hard to choose dark, medium, and light colors, (value) though working with many hues. With the block variations and the hand-dyed fabrics, this piece has the look of a painting. An art quilt! The results are outstanding. Pieced and machine quilted by Jean Look-Krischano.

All Nations Wall Hanging; 27½" x 32". Dividing this hexagon into three diamond-shaped areas of different values (a light pieced diamond, a medium pieced diamond, and a dark pieced diamond) produces the illusion of a cube, even though the star designs still stand out. All 60° triangle designs have a potential for 3-D effects. Sara and Joan worked on color and value together. Bright colors and simple shapes are reminiscent of flags. Even the hanging itself is a flag shape. Pieced by Joan Dawson and hand-quilted by Sara Nephew.

Frogs And Lightning; 72" x 81". Can you see the reason for the name of this quilt? Some of the shapes reminded the author of Native American geometric motifs, like those on pottery or in rugs. Colors were chosen for a western look. Solid fabrics achieved the look of Southwest art better than prints would. To produce the frog and lightning motifs, it is necessary to color the quilt diagram and use it as a piecing chart. Each diagonal row of blocks has four identically colored blocks in it. Once the main part of the design was laid out, colors were chosen to finish the upper right and bottom left areas.

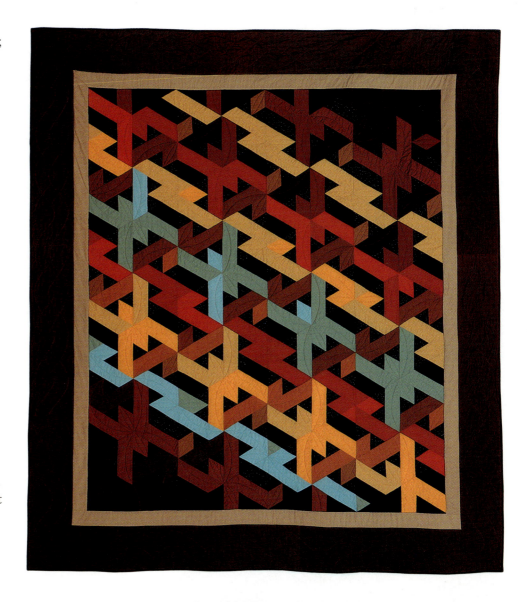

Blooming Garden; 91½" x 97¼". Maybe influenced by the pattern title, Eda made brightly colored flowers and raindrops on leaves with her fabric choices. (Perhaps a natural choice for someone from the Pacific Northwest.) Using intense bright colors produces a strong design, of stars and interlocking circles. The colors and shapes are reminiscent of illuminated pages in medieval manuscripts. A strong design is enclosed in a strong border. The gold inner border and the green outer border are sewn into a strip set, and both are cut at once to the correct length. (A little math is necessary.) The pieced borders are then sewn on in order clockwise, with the first seam finished after the final section has been added. Pieced by Eda Haas.

Rosedance; 89½" x 103". Changing colors and values in the setting triangle produce three quilts in one. The top section of the quilt is in lighter colors and emphasizes lacy interlocking circles. The middle area has rings of bright colors. In the bottom panel large stars appear. Other effects are possible. What if all the values were reversed? If you choose to fast-piece the "stripped triangles" used in every block and alternate block, there will be triangles from the other side of the set of strips to use in the "Two Step" quilt.

Little Star; 28" x 31¾". When the author started piecing "Nova" and held a small center star in her hand, this quilt was born. Pastels and diminutive floral prints make a soft impression. Hand quilted by Sara Nephew.

Native Star; 47¼" x 50½". This first Showcase quilt reminded the author of Plains Indian star quilts. Beautiful machine quilting in the white space gives it a luxurious feel. What other block and star points would look good with this border?

Sparks; 52¼" x 66¾". Diane captured all the excitement and motion of this design with value choices and graded shading. Notice the lighter vertical center area. Pieced by Diane Coombs and machine quilted by Barbara Dau.

Rain Of Stars; 73" x 88¾", is an easy and fast quilt to piece. Large light triangles alternate with a pieced setting triangle and **Voila!**, stars are created. Careful placement of some medium values adds interest to the design. This quilt is a sampler of Marsha McCloskey's Staples™ fabric collection. Machine quilted by Lynnette Baxter.

Oriental; 40" x 44", is the second Showcase Quilt. Different choice of block and star points calls for a very different border. The left and right inner borderextend to the edge of the piecing to add an interesting emphasis to the design. This quilt is pieced almost completely from Mission Valley fabrics.

Blizzard; 42¼" x 45½". The third Showcase Quilt features a combination of many triangles with busy, swirling prints to bring out the idea of snowflakes. It looks cold, but would surely make a good lap quilt.

Sparks; 50" x 64½", pieced by Lessa Siegele, has a very different look from the one made by Diane. The dark background sets off the hexagon blocks and creates large stars. Hot colors and agate-like prints play against cool deep-sea blues.(above left)

Bunkhouse Blanket; 86" x 97¼". Look for a badge and western belt in the light diagonal bands of the design. Hues echo pine trees, sand and rocks. Even the prints are western themes. It looked great on my bed! Pieced and machine quilted by Judy Rein. (above right)

Two Step; 78" x 89¼". Two easy pieced triangle units inspired the name of this quick quilt. Leftover alternate stripped triangles from the "Rosedance" quilt made it even faster. A mix of prints combines with large diamonds of Mission Valley woven plaids.(right)

Nova; 62" x 71". The author began by deciding to use a red, white and blue color scheme with graded shading. After the blocks were about two thirds pieced, they were laid out on the floor. The quilt was too busy, jumbled and uncontrollable, until diagonal graded bands of alternating red and blue were tried. Now there is just enough organization to allow the eye to travel from one point of interest to another in a pleasing visual experience. "Stars and Stripes Forever!"

RAIN OF STARS

3" triangle size
Quilt with borders: 73" x 88¾"

All fabric 42" prewashed.
Fabric requirements:
2½ yds. dark fabrics
4 yds. light fabrics

Directions:
1. For each triangle block, cut:

3	dark	2¾"	diamond
3	light	3"	triangle

Assemble as shown in the diagram. Make 86 blocks altogether. Cut 85 light 7½" triangles for the Alternate Block.

Rain of Stars Block

Piecing Diagram

Alternate Block

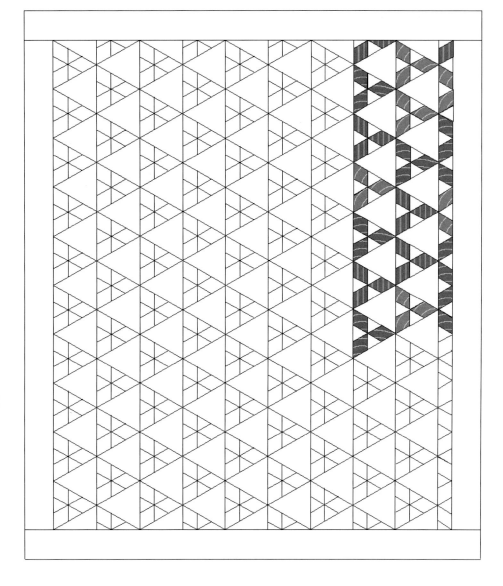

2. Assemble in vertical rows as shown. Finish the top and bottom of five rows with a light triangle half cut from an 8" triangle. Complete the other four rows with a left or right finishing piece assembled from:

1	dark	2¾"	diamond
1	dark	3"	triangle
1	dark	1⅞"	diamond half
1	light	3½"	triangle half (from triangle)

Left Finishing Piece   Right Finishing Piece

3. Complete the pattern with a border of dark diamonds and light triangles on the right side of the quilt as shown, finished top and bottom with a 3½" light triangle half. Add a final 5¼" border.

ACAPULCO SUN

3" triangle size
Quilt without borders: 31½" x 53"

All fabric 42" wide prewashed.
Fabric requirements:
½ yd. dark fabrics for blocks
½ yd. light fabrics for blocks
½ yd. medium fabrics for blocks
⅓ yd. light fabric for setting triangle halves
⅓ yd. medium fabric for setting triangle halves
⅛ yd. dark fabric for setting triangle halves
⅓ yd. fabric for setting triangles
1¼ yds. border fabric

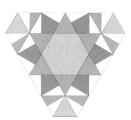

Sew the correct pieced flat pyramids on three sides of each Sunflower block to make four larger triangles.

Sew the correct strips on three sides of each larger triangle to make all four 3-Row blocks.

Directions:
1. Make four Sunflower blocks according to the directions on pg. 6.

2. Cut and add pieces to the Sunflower blocks to make four 3-Row blocks: *(Complete the last row of each as in the blocks below.)*

A. Complete as Cut Paper Star, pg. 8. Cut:

6	3"	dark	triangle
6	2¾"	light	diamond
12	3½"	sandwich-pieced half-triangle	

Make six pieced flat pyramids as shown. Sew three of them onto the Sunflower block to make a larger triangle. Make three strips as shown. Sew on three sides of the larger triangle to make a hexagon block.

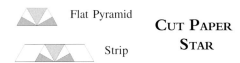

CUT PAPER STAR

B. Complete as in the Circus block, pg. 14. Cut:

6	dark	3"	triangle
6	light	3"	triangle
6	light	5¼"	flat pyramid (2¾" strip)

Make six pieced flat pyramids as shown. Sew three of them onto the Sunflower block to make a larger triangle. Make three strips as shown. Sew on three sides of the larger triangle to make a hexagon block.

CIRCUS

C. Complete as in the Facets block, pg. 9. Cut:

6	dark	3"	triangle
12	light	3"	triangle
6	medium	2¾"	diamond

Make six pieced flat pyramids as shown. Sew three of them onto the Sunflower block to make a larger triangle. Make three strips as shown. Sew on three sides of the larger triangle to make a hexagon block.

FACETS

D. Complete as in the Radiant Star block, pg. 10. (Even though Radiant Star has a triangle center, the Sunflower block substitutes for this.) Cut:

6	dark	3"	triangle
12	light	3"	triangle
6	dark	3⅜"	teardrop
12	light	3½"	triangle half

Make six flat pyramids as shown. Sew three of them onto the Sunflower block to make a larger triangle. Make three strips as shown. Sew on three sides of the larger triangle to make a hexagon block.

RADIANT STAR

ACAPULCO SUN

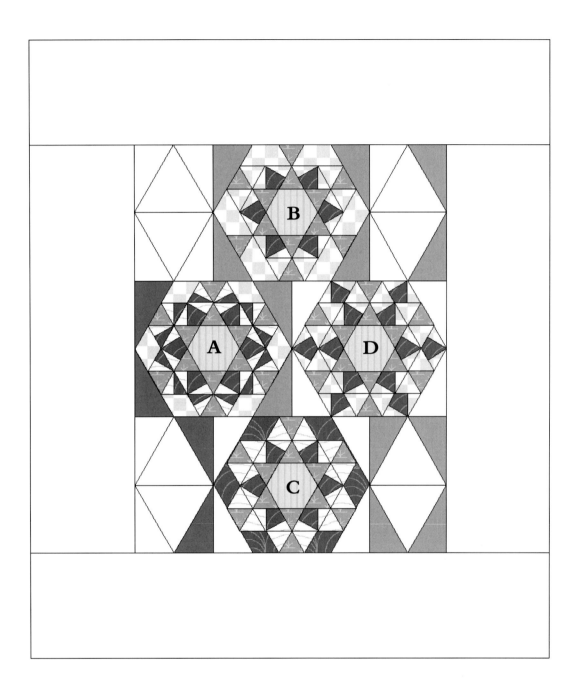

3. Cut:

16	light	8"	triangle half ★
12	medium	8"	triangle half ★
4	dark	8"	triangle half ★
8	light	7½"	triangle

★ Cut from 8" triangle.

Choose colors and values for all these pieces to complement the blocks you have created.

Add the triangle halves to the blocks to make rectangles according to the values shown in the quilt diagram, or your preference. Sew the 7½" triangles together in two's to make diamonds and frame them with triangle halves to make rectangles as shown in the quilt diagram. Sew together the blocks and rectangles to make three rows as shown, or according to your preference. Sew the rows together and add a 6½" border to complete the quilt.

BLOOMING GARDEN

3" triangle size
Quilt with borders: 81½" x 87¼"

All fabric 42" wide prewashed.
Fabric requirements:
3 yds. floral fabric (mixed)
1 yd. star point fabric
1¼ yds. yellow fabric
1⅔ yds. white diamond fabric
2½ yds. setting hexagons
¾ yd. setting triangles
½ yd. inner border fabric
2¼ yds. border fabric

Directions:
1. Make 27 Blooming Star blocks according to the directions on pg. 8.

2. Make 66 setting triangles.
For each setting triangle cut:

1	light	5"	hexagon
3	green	3"	triangle

3. Make six partial blocks.
For each partial block cut:

4	floral	5¼"	flat pyramid (2¾"strip)
2	floral	5"	long diamond (2¾" strip)
1	floral	2¾"	diamond
1	yellow	5"	hexagon
6	star	3"	triangle
1	floral	1⅞"	diamond half
2	white	5¾"	triangle half (left/right)

Assemble according to the diagram. Sew on a setting triangle as shown.

4. Make six fill-in pieces. Cut six diamond halves from a 4⅝" strip of background fabric. Sew onto a setting triangle as shown.

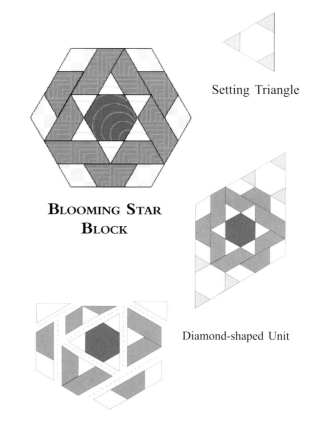

BLOOMING STAR BLOCK

Setting Triangle

Diamond-shaped Unit

Piecing Diagram For Partial Block

PARTIAL BLOCK

FILL-IN PIECE

5. Sew two setting triangles onto each block to make a diamond-shaped unit. Assemble four blocks and two partial blocks into a vertical row. Make three of these. Assemble five blocks and two fill-in pieces into a vertical row. Make three of these. Sew the two rows together alternately according to the quilt diagram. Eda added a 1½" inner border and a final 9½" outer border to complete the quilt.

BLOOMING GARDEN

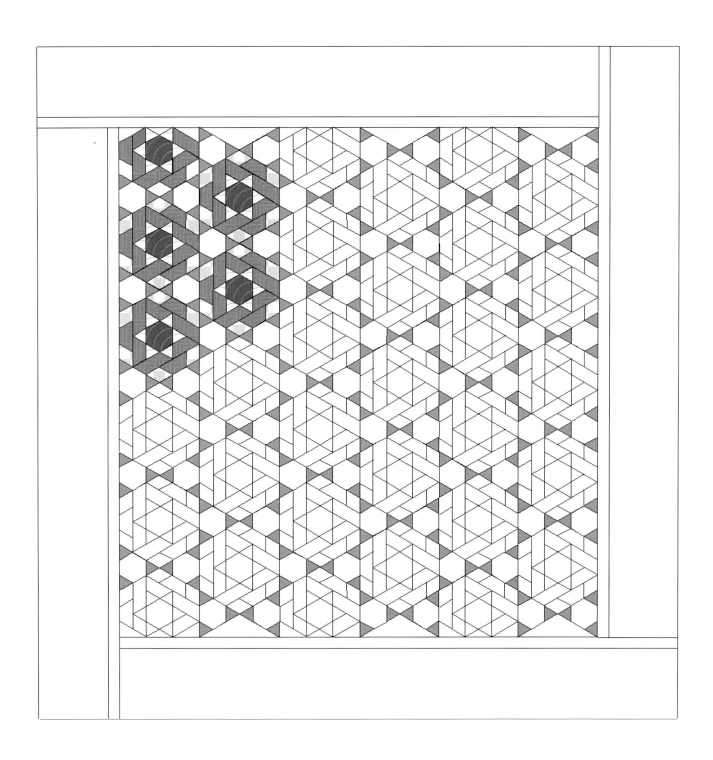

37

SYMPHONY

All fabric 42" wide prewashed.
Fabric Requirements:
2 yds. each light medium and dark fabrics (start with an assortment of ¼ yd. cuts of blue, white, pink and lavender)

Directions:
1. Make 16 Star Surrounded blocks according to the directions on pg. 5. Then make pieced triangles as shown. For each one cut:

2	light	3"	triangle
1	dark	2¾"	diamond

Make 104 of these. Sew three pieced triangles on each Star Surrounded block to make a Symphony block.

2. Make 32 Checkerboard Diamonds.
A. Cut one light and one dark 2¾" strip. Sew together lengthwise. Cut the ends of the strips to a 60° angle as shown in the diagram and cut 2¾" pairs of diamonds from the set of strips, checking the angle occasionally. Sew into Checkerboard Diamonds as shown. You will need 56 altogether.

3. Assemble the Alternate Block from three Checkerboard Diamonds and three pieced triangles as shown in the diagram. Make 16.

4. For each Left or Right Star Half-block cut:

1	dark	1⅞"	diamond half
3	both	1⅞"	½-diamond (sandwich-pieced)
4	light	3"	triangle
1	light	3½"	triangle half
1	light	8"	triangle half

Add a pieced triangle and assemble as shown. Make two of each.

5. Cut:

1	dark	2¾"	diamond
1	dark	1⅞"	diamond half
2	light	1⅞"	diamond half
1	light	3"	triangle

6. Add one Checkerboard Diamond and one pieced triangle and assemble a Left or Right Alternate Half-block. Make two of each. Arrange the blocks into five rows. Finish the ends of the rows with pieced half-blocks. Then sew the rows together. Add a 6" final border to complete the quilt.

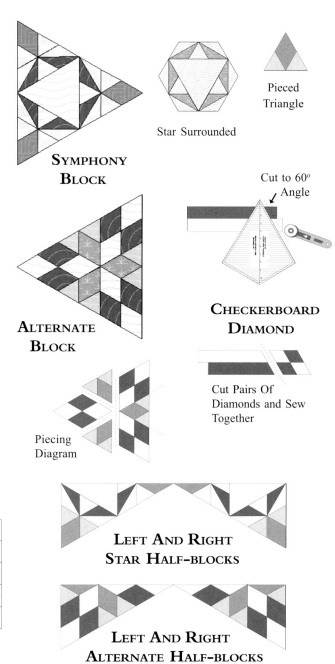

3" triangle size
Quilt with borders: 63½" x 79"

SYMPHONY

FROGS AND LIGHTNING

> **3" triangle size**
> Quilt without borders: 72" x 81"

All fabric 42" wide prewashed.
Fabric Requirements:
¾ yds. each green, red, yellow, and brown fabrics
1½ yds. black fabric
¾ yd. inner border fabric
1½ yds. outer border fabric

Directions:
1. Make 12 Twist Tie blocks according to the directions on pg. 7. In addition, 16 extra wedges will be needed. (You may wish to color the quilt diagram so you have a piecing chart to follow.)

2. To make each of the 32 setting triangles cut:

1	light	3"	triangle
1	dark	5¼"	flat pyramid (2¾" strip)
1	light	7½"	flat pyramid (2¾" strip)

(OR: If you don't need careful control of color, sew two 3" light strips and one 2¾" dark strip together lengthwise into a strata. Cut 7¾" triangles from this set of strips. Trim ¼" from the bottom of each triangle. Sew setting triangles on opposite sides of each block to make a complete diamond-shaped block.

2. Cut for the partial blocks and fill-in pieces:

8	dark	triangle half (4⅝" x 8" rectangle A)
8	dark	triangle half (3⅜" x 5¾" rectangle B)
8	light	long quarter hex (2¾" x 4⅝" rectangle)

Cut the rectangle for the triangle half at an angle as shown.

A

B

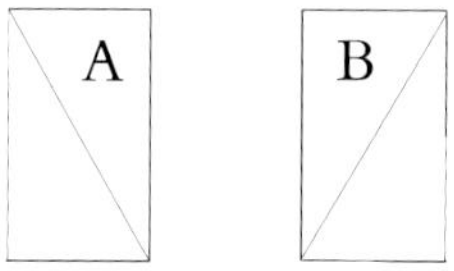

3. Sew the quarter hex to the dark triangle half as shown to make a pieced triangle half.

Pieced triangle half

B

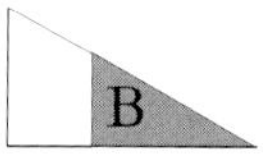

Use four Twist Tie wedges, a pieced triangle half and a medium 8" triangle half for each partial block. Assemble according to the diagram. Make four.

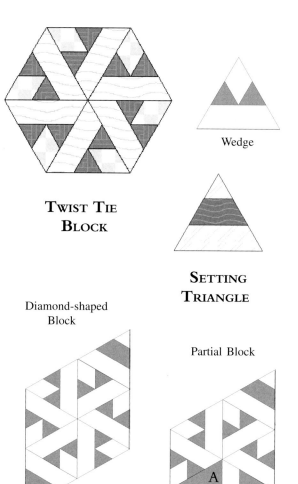

Twist Tie Block

Wedge

Setting Triangle

Diamond-shaped Block

Partial Block

A

Half-Triangle B

4. Use a setting triangle, a pieced triangle half and a medium 8" triangle half for each fill-in piece. Assemble as shown. Make four of these.

Fill-in piece
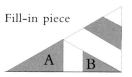

5. Make four rows of three complete blocks each. Finish the top and bottom of each row alternately with partial blocks and fill-in pieces according to the diagram. Then sew the rows together. Add a 2¾" inner border and a 7" final border to complete the quilt.

FROGS AND LIGHTNING

BUNKHOUSE BLANKET

All fabric 42" wide prewashed.
Fabric Requirements:
½ yd. each of 3 different blues, greens, reds
1 yd. each 3 different beige fabrics
½ yd. inner border fabric
2¼ yds. outer border fabric

3" triangle size
Quilt without borders: 86" x 97¼"

Directions:
1. Make 20 Sheriff's Star blocks according to the directions on pg. 9.

2. To make the setting triangles cut:

1	dark	3"	triangle
1	light	5¼"	flat pyramid (2¾" strip)
1	dark	7½"	flat pyramid (2¾" strip)

(OR: sew two 3" dark strips and one 2¾" light strip together lengthwise into a strata as shown. Press to the light. Cut 7¾" triangles from this set of strips. **Trim ¼" from the bottom of each triangle to make 7½" triangles.** You will need 50 setting triangles altogether.) Sew two setting triangles on opposite sides of a Sheriff's Star block to make a complete block. Make 20 of these.

3. Cut for partial blocks:

8	dark	2¾"	diamonds
4	light	5¼"	flat pyramids (2¾" strip)
1	dark	1⅞"	diamond half
2	dark	3½"	triangle half (1 left/1 right)

Assemble according to the diagram.

4. Cut six light diamond halves from a 4⅝" strip. Move the **Super 60** along the line to cut, or extend the line with another ruler. Sew to a setting triangle as shown to make a fill-in piece.

5. Assemble the quilt top in five rows with four blocks and one partial block in each row. Finish the other end with a fill-in piece as shown in the quilt diagram. Add a 2" inner border and a final 8" outer border to complete the quilt.

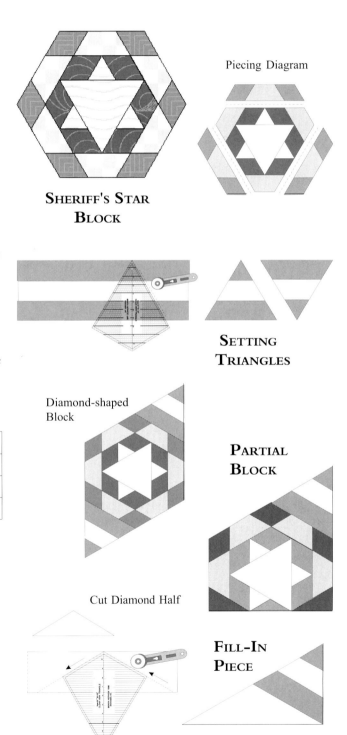

Sheriff's Star Block

Piecing Diagram

Setting Triangles

Diamond-shaped Block

Partial Block

Cut Diamond Half

Fill-In Piece

BUNKHOUSE BLANKET

NOVA

3" triangle size
Quilt without borders: 62" x 71½"

Directions:
1. Cut for one Little Star:

1	dark	4⅛"	triangle
3	dark	1⅞"	triangle
6	light	1⅝"	diamond

Assemble according to the diagram. Make 16 of these. Using the Little Stars, make 12 Circus blocks according to the directions on pg. 14. Use the remaining Little Stars in the partial blocks below.

2. Cut for one setting triangle:

3	dark	2¾"	diamond
3	light	3"	triangle

Assemble the setting triangle according to the diagram. Make 32 of these. Sew setting triangles on opposite sides of the Circus blocks to make complete diamond-shaped blocks. You will have eight left over.

3. Cut for one partial block:

5	dark	2¾"	diamond
11	light	3"	triangle
4	dark	3"	triangle
1	dark	1⅞"	diamond half
3	light	5¼"	flat pryamid (2¾" strip)
2	light	5¾"	triangle half (1 right/1 left)

Assemble as shown, using a Little Star from #1 above, and one setting triangle. Make four of these.

4. Cut four light diamond halves from a 4⅝" strip. (See pg. 42.) Sew a setting triangle onto each one as shown to make four fill-in pieces.

5. Assemble three blocks, a partial block, and a fill-in piece into a vertical row with the fill-in piece on the top and the partial block on the bottom of the row. Make two of these. Make two rows with the fill-in piece on the bottom and the partial blocks on the top. Sew the rows together and add a final 4" border to complete the quilt.

All fabric 42" wide prewashed.
Fabric Requirements:
½ yd. each light and dark fabric for little star
1½ yd. each light and dark fabric for blocks
½ yd. light fabric for setting triangles
1 yd. dark fabric for setting triangles
1 yd. border fabric

CIRCUS BLOCK

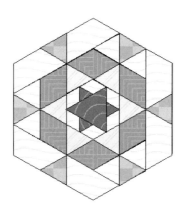

LITTLE STAR

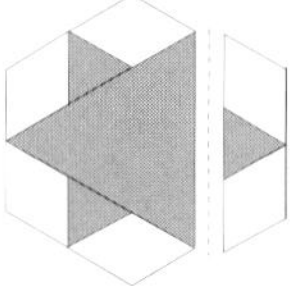

Piecing Diagram

Diamond-Shaped Block

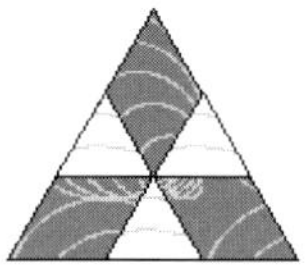

SETTING TRIANGLE

PARTIAL BLOCK

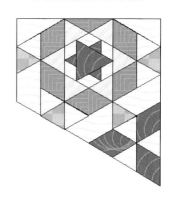

Piecing Diagram

FILL-IN PIECE

NOVA

ROSEDANCE

3" triangle size
Quilt with borders: 89½" x 103"

All fabric 42" wide prewashed.
Fabric Requirements:
2 yds. each brown and white fabric for stripped triangles (3⅓ yds. if strip-piecing as in #1)
2 yds. fabric for diamonds
1 yd. each hexagon fabric and block triangle fabric
1¼ yds. each purple and pastel (Setting block half-diamonds)
1¼ yds. each pink and red (**Rosedance** block half-diamonds)
1¼ yds. border fabric

Directions: *If you made Twostep, you already have some of these stripped triangles.*

1. Cut a 3" triangle and a 5¼" flat pyramid (2¾" strip) and sew these together to make the stripped triangle. You will need 222 for Rosedance. Or: Sew 3" selvage-to-selvage strips of light and dark fabric together lengthwise. (30 sets of strips) Cut 5½" triangles from this set of strips. Trim ¼" from the bottom of each triangle. Sort into pieced triangles with a dark tip (for **Rosedance**) and pieced triangles with a light tip (for **Twostep**).

2. Sandwich-piece half-diamonds from 1⅞" light and dark strips. You will need 216 half-diamonds for the Rosedance quilt. (18 sets of strips)

3. Make 33 Wood Rose blocks, pg. 5. Add three dark-tipped triangles as shown in the piecing diagram to make the Rosedance block.

4. Cut 216 light diamonds (from a 2¾" strip). Assemble a diamond unit as shown from two diamonds and two half-diamonds. Make 105 of these. Use three diamond units and three dark-tipped stripped triangles to make the Alternate block. Make 33 of these. (above right)

5. Assemble left and right partial blocks from:

1	diamond unit
2	stripped triangle
1	half-diamond
2	light diamond half (1⅞" strip)

Sew on a stripped triangle and trim even with other pieces. (can use leftover strip ends) Make three left and three right partial blocks.

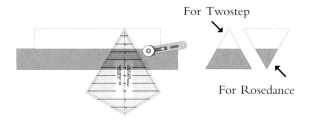

STRIPPED TRIANGLES
For Twostep
For Rosedance

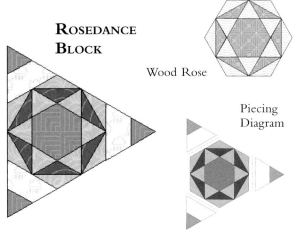

ROSEDANCE BLOCK

Wood Rose

Piecing Diagram

ALTERNATE BLOCK

Diamond Unit

Piecing Diagram

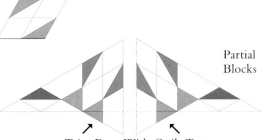

Partial Blocks

Trim Even With Quilt Top

ROSEDANCE

6. Assemble fill-in pieces from two light 5" x 5¾" rectangles *(place right sides together and trim one short end to a 60° angle as shown)*, and one stripped triangle. Add a stripped triangle at the right or left side. (You can use imperfect ones from end of strata.) Trim even. Make three left and three right fill-in pieces.

7. Assemble 11 block triangles and 11 alternate triangles into two rows (first on the left as shown in the quilt diagram), adding partial blocks and fill-in pieces at top and bottom as required. Make three of these vertical panels and sew them together to make the quilt top. Add a final 4½" border to complete the quilt.

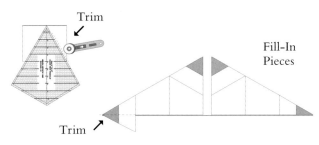

SPARKS

3" triangle size
Quilt without borders: 52¼" x 66¾"

All fabric 42" wide prewashed.
Fabric Requirements:
2 yds. each light, medium, and dark fabrics (a mix of many fabrics)
½ yd. inner border fabric
1 yd. outer border fabric

Directions:

1. Make 8 Chain blocks according to the directions on pg. 11.

2. To make one setting triangle cut:

3	dark	3"	triangle
1	light	5"	hexagon

Assemble according to the diagram. Make 22.

SETTING TRIANGLE

3. Assemble each partial block from:

3	Chain Units
1	light 5" hexagon
1	each of pieces A, B, C

Cut for A:

2	dark	2¾"	diamond
1	light	3"	triangle
1	light	5¾"	triangle half

A.

Cut for B:

1	dark	quarter hex ★
★ 2¾" x 3⅜" rectangle		
1	light	3½"	triangle half

B.

Cut for C:

1	dark	2¾"	diamond
2	light	3"	triangles
1	light	5¾"	triangle half

C.

Partial Block Piecing Diagram

Finish This Seam Last

Sew Fill-in piece A onto one side of the hexagon, leaving 1" of the seam open. Sew on Fill-in piece B and C in order. Then add the three Chain units onto the next three clockwise sides of the hexagon. Finally finish sewing the first seam. Make two partial blocks.

4. Cut six light diamond halves from a 4⅝" strip. (See pg. 42.) Sew to a setting triangle as shown to make a finishing piece. Make four.

FINISHING PIECE

5. Assemble the quilt top in three rows according to the quilt diagram. Add a 2¾" inner border and a final 5" outer border to complete the quilt.

CUTTING DIRECTIONS

Tools

This book features a new tool, the Super 60. The Super 60 combines the most versatile Clearview Triangle, the 8" Mini-Pro, with the ½-diamond, so with one new tool you can cut every shape needed in this book. (Sometimes a cut will need to be extended with another ruler, to make a larger piece. See pg. 54.)

Both the Super 60 and all the Clearview Triangles are made from ⅛" thick acrylic for use with a rotary cutter. (See pg. 56 for ordering information.) You may already own the two tools mentioned above. If so, you will not need the new tool. Just use the 8" triangle when directions refer to "the narrow end" and the ½-diamond when directions refer to "the wide end".

Besides Clearview Triangles, required tools are: rotary cutter, mat, and a straight ruler like Omnigrid (they now have new line and dot markings which are even easier to use) for cutting strips. Use the size of rotary cutter you prefer, although the smallest is better for cutting around curves (like cutting out clothing patterns), and the two larger sizes save muscle strain, cut faster, and tend to stay on a straight line. A 6" x 12" ruler moves less while cutting.

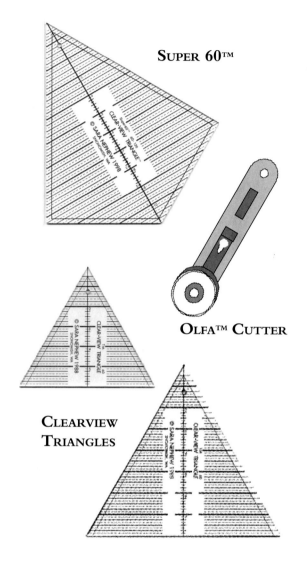

SUPER 60™

OLFA™ CUTTER

CLEARVIEW TRIANGLES

Rotary Cutting and Speed Piecing

These cutting methods are based on:
1. a strip of fabric;
2. a plastic 60° triangle tool with a ruled line on the perpendicular. The tool is laid on the strip in various ways, and a rotary cutter is used to cut off portions of the fabric strip. Nothing in this book is difficult to do as long as the triangle tool and the strip are kept in mind. By working just with these elements, many shapes can be cut in whatever size is desired. These shapes will all fit together to form a quilt top. The following section lists the methods for cutting the shapes used in this book. The index on pg. 55 makes it easy to find a shape, so you can review cutting methods while piecing a particular pattern.

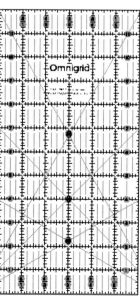

OMNIGRID™
6" x 12"

Many Shapes

To cut a strip:

The first step in cutting any shape is to cut a strip. All fabric should be prewashed. 100% cotton is best.

1. Fold fabric selvage to selvage and press. If pressing from the selvage to the fold produces wrinkles, move the top layer of fabric left or right keeping selvages parallel, until wrinkles disappear.
2. Bring fold to selvage (folding again) and press.
3. Use the wide ruler as a right angle guide, or line up the selvages with the edge of the mat, and the ruler with the mat edge perpendicular to the selvage. Cut off the ragged or irregular edges of the fabric.
4. Cut the strip width required, using the newly trimmed fabric edge as a guide.
5. Open the strip. It should be straight, not zigzag. Adjust the ruler if necessary and trim fabric edges slightly before cutting the next strip.

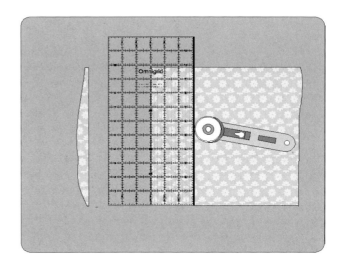

Trim ragged edge from twice-folded fabric. Then begin to cut strips. Use a wide ruler (or lines on the mat) to line up cuts.

To cut a triangle (3" triangle size):

1. Cut a 3" strip.
2. Position the narrow end of the Super 60 at one edge of the strip and the 3" line at the other edge of the strip.
3. Rotary cut along both sides of the triangle. Move the tool along the same edge (do not flip it to the other side of the fabric strip) for the next cut. Line up the tool again as shown.
4. Cut along both sides of the triangle. Strips may be stacked up to 8 thicknesses and all cut at once.

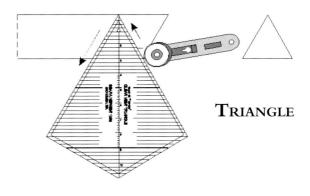

TRIANGLE

To cut a diamond (3" triangle size):

1. Cut a 2¾" strip. (Or cut whatever size strip the directions call for.)
2. Position the Super 60 (narrow end up) with one side along one edge of the strip. Cut the end of the strip to a 60° angle.
3. Reposition the Super 60 so the tip is at one edge of the strip and a ruled line is along the other edge. (The same position as is used to cut triangles, except the strip is ¼" narrower.)
4. Rotary cut **only** along the side opposite the first cut.
5. Keep moving the tool along the same side of the strip, lining up the cut edge and the side of the tool as shown. Always cut the side opposite the first cut. (Strips may be stacked up to 8 thicknesses and all cut at once.)

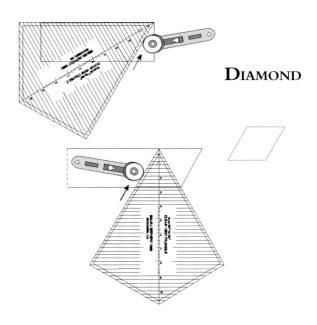

DIAMOND

To cut a long diamond (3" triangle size):
1. Cut a 2¾" strip.
2. Trim one end of the strip to a 60° angle.
3. Place the Super 60 over the fabric strip as shown. Set the bottom edge of the strip at the measurement given in the pattern (usually 5"). Cut the side opposite the first cut.

Note: Care must be taken when cutting long diamonds, as they do have a reverse of their shape. Check carefully to be sure you are cutting them in the direction required by the pattern. If you don't need both the long diamond and its reverse, keep fabric right sides up. Try cutting just one first, to be sure it's right.

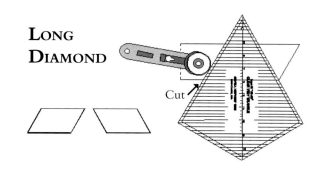

LONG DIAMOND

To cut a flat pyramid (3" triangle size):
1. Cut a 2¾" strip.
2. Place the narrow end of the Super 60 over the fabric strip, lining up the bottom edge of the strip at the measurement given in the pattern (usually 5¼"). Cut each side of the strip.

Note: Turn the Super 60 and cut the next flat pyramid from the other side of the strip to save fabric.

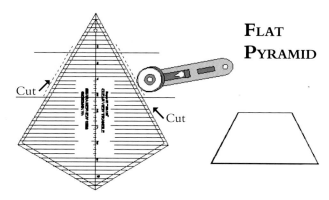

FLAT PYRAMID

To cut a triangle half (3" triangle size):

Method #1
1. Cut triangles from a 3½" strip.
2. Line up the side of the fabric triangle with the perpendicular line on the narrow end of the Super 60. Cut the fabric triangle in half along the edge of the tool.

Method #2
1. Cut a rectangle the height needed for the triangle half (2" x 3½").
2. Using the narrow end of the Super 60, bisect this rectangle from corner to corner diagonally. (This will produce two halves the same, rather than a left and a right. Lay the ruler from corner to corner to check and see if this is the shape needed. If not, lay it along the other two corners. To get left and right halves, lay two rectangles right or wrong sides together.)

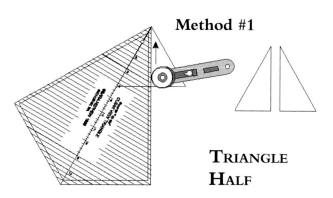

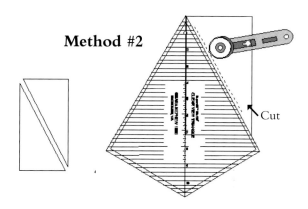

TRIANGLE HALF

51

To cut a diamond half (3" triangle size):

Method #1
Use the wide end of the Super 60 to rotary cut wide triangles from the proper width strip (usually 1⅞").

Method #2 (Using a Clearview Triangle)
1. Line up center line of the tool with the edge of the fabric strip.
2. Flip or turn the tool, line up the center line with strip edge and previous cut at edge of tool. Cut other 30° angle.

To cut a teardrop (3" triangle size):
Method #1
1. Cut triangles from a 3⅜" strip.
2. Position Super 60 on triangle with the perpendicular on the top point of the triangle, the other two corners lined up evenly with one of the rulings, and the wide angle just at or inside the bottom edge as shown. Cut the base of the teardrop.

Method #2 (Using a Clearview Triangle)
1. Cut triangles from a 3⅜" strip.
2. Measure the base of these triangles and find the center or half measurement.
3. Lay the perpendicular of the Clearview Triangle along the base of the fabric triangle, with the point at center. Rotary cut this wedge off. Reverse the tool and cut off the other wedge.

Teardrop Unit
A teardrop unit, made from one teardrop shape and two triangle halves, is very useful. Seam one triangle half on each side of the teardrop to make a diamond-shaped unit. I line these pieces up for seaming at the bottom, not the top. Press each seam. Trim off the little seam ears to finish. Then press, pressing the seam allowances away from the teardrop shape. Trim off the little seam ears as shown.

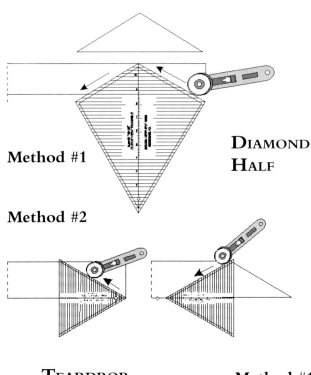

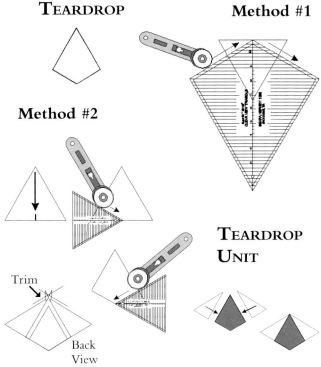

To cut a quarter hex (3" triangle size):
1. Cut a 2¾" strip.
2. Cut 3⅜" sections from the strip.
3. Position the Super 60 with one side along the long edge of the strip. Trim to a 60° angle. This piece does have a reverse. Check to be sure which shape you need.

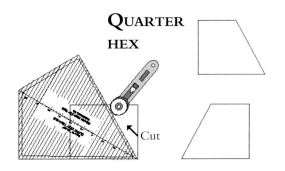

To cut a hexagon (3" triangle size):
1. Cut a 5" strip.
2. Cut 60° diamonds from the 5" strip. (See "To cut diamonds," pg. 50).
3. From each end of the diamond, cut a 2½" triangle.

To cut a gem shape (3" triangle size):
Instead of cutting a hexagon from the diamond, cut only one point off, leaving this shape.

Sandwich-piecing
(Sandwich-piecing uses two strips of fabric.)

To sandwich-piece a matching triangle (3" triangle size):
1. Cut 3" strips. Two different fabrics are used, usually one light and one dark. Seam these strips right sides together with a ¼" seam down both the right and the left side of the pair of strips. Cut triangles from this set of strips.
2. Pull the tips of the seamed triangles apart and press.

To sandwich-piece a ½-diamond (3" triangle size):
This piece requires careful attention, both in cutting and seaming. If too small, a narrower seam width is the solution. If too large, a wider seam.

1. Cut strips of fabric according to the pattern (usually 1⅞"). Two different fabrics are used, usually one light and one dark.
2. Sew light and dark strips right sides together with a ¼" seam allowance down each side.
3. Using the Super 60 and a rotary cutter, cut triangles from the seamed strips. Line up the wide tool tip at one seamed edge, and the desired line on the ruler at the other edge, and cut as for triangles.
4. Use a seam ripper to cut one stitch at the seamed tip of the half-diamonds.
5. Pull the tips apart and press.

Method #2 (Using a Clearview Triangle)
Cut the half-diamond as for cutting diamond halves, pg. 52.

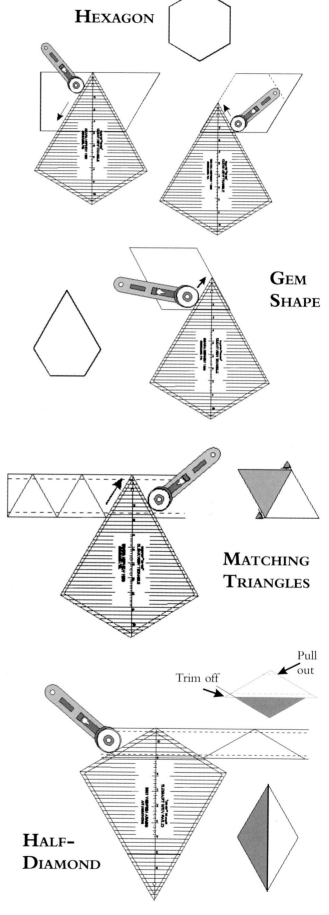

To sandwich-piece a ½-triangle (3" triangle size):
1. Cut two 2" fabric strips. Usually a dark and a light are used. Press these right sides together.
2. Seam through both strips ¼" away on both sides of all the lines drawn. Press flat again.
3. Cut 3½" sections from the strips.
4. Bisect sections diagonally by lining up the center line of the Super 60 with the long edge of the section, narrow point at the top edge. Line up at the left or right to get the half-triangle you need, or place sections right or wrong sides together (instead of same fabric up) to get both kinds. Pull tips apart and press.

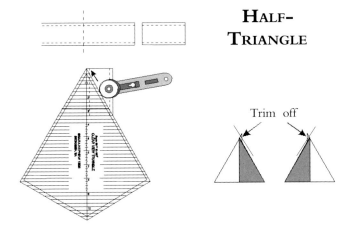

HALF-TRIANGLE

Trim off

Cutting Large Shapes

No matter how large a triangle ruler you are using, sooner or later you will find yourself faced with the task of cutting a shape even larger. Don't be intimidated by the idea. Remember, you are dealing with only a small number of possible angles in 60° quilts (30°, 60°, or 120°), and they are easy to recognize. There are two relatively simple ways to approach this cutting challenge.

First Method

Cut a strip the height of the triangle. Then cut the angles needed. To cut a large equilateral triangle (60° at all three corners) use the narrow end of the Super 60 to get an accurate angle at the first corner. Then either extend the side with a long straight ruler or move the Super 60 along the cut edge to continue. Cut the next corner accurately and continue until the shape is finished.

For a large diamond half, see pg. 52. Remember, the larger the piece you are cutting, the less difference small variations will make to the unit's comfortable fit in the quilt top.

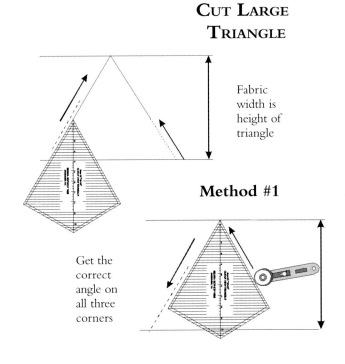

CUT LARGE TRIANGLE

Fabric width is height of triangle

Method #1

Get the correct angle on all three corners

Method #2

Second Method

The second approach is to add ruler height to the Clearview Triangle that you have in order to make it a larger triangle (sort of). To cut a large triangle out if any piece of fabric, first make a straight cut along one edge of the fabric. Put the bottom edge of the Clearview Triangle on this straight fabric edge. Then use a ruler to add the necessary inches, pushing the triangle up. Cut the left and right sides by either laying a long ruler down or by moving the Clearview Triangle and continuing the cut.

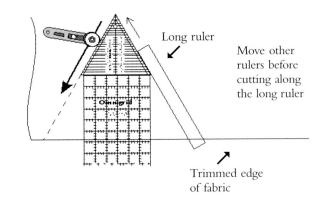

Long ruler

Move other rulers before cutting along the long ruler

Trimmed edge of fabric

Piecing Hints

All my piecing is done with a ¼" seam. Even if the presser foot on your sewing machine features this ¼" for you, it is a good idea to measure the seams occasionally until you are confident of accuracy. Check to be sure the seam is just inside the ¼" line rather than right on it.

When many seams intersect at one point, pinch the center where the seams cross, open the fabric to see how the seams are meeting and adjust as necessary. Pin to hold the fabric for seaming.

A few tips about trimming seams are illustrated in these cutting instructions. I trim in a number of places to reduce bulk as the quilt top is pieced. Be careful not to trim too much off before the next step, however, as the little points that stick out help align the parts for accurate sewing. Experience helps. The mild bias of the triangles also aids in lining up seams. Pull a little if necessary. All seams are pressed to one side to make quilting easier.

Index of Shapes

Strip	50
Triangle	50
Diamond	50
Long Diamond	51
Flat Pyramid	51
Triangle Half	51
Diamond Half	52
Teardrop	52
Quarter Hex	52
Hexagon	53
Gem Shape	53
Sandwich-piecing	53
Matching Triangles	53
Half-diamonds	53
Half-triangle	54
Large Triangle	54

SARA NEPHEW

Sara Nephew graduated from Alverno College in Milwaukee, WI, with an art major. She was trained as a jeweler, and showed her cloisonne' enamel work in national shows. She began her first quilt in 1967, using corduroy squares from her daughters rompers. In the 80's she began to apply her art training seriously to quilting and in 1984 started a business making and repairing quilts.

She has since originated a series of tools for rotary cutting isometric shapes, authored 12 books, and become an internationally known teacher and lecturer.

Sara now lives in Clearview, WA, with her husband, Dale. She is enjoying her three grown children and her two granddaughters. Dale is retired, and he helps in the quilting business. The couple have taken up birdwatching as another interest.

OTHER PRODUCTS FROM CLEARVIEW TRIANGLE

New Series - Quick Picture Quilts

ZO 18	$24.95	Book - Patchwork Zoo	plus $3.00 s/h
HH-17	9.95	Book - Happy Halloween	plus 2.00 s/h
NL-19	6.95	Book - New Labels	plus 2.00 s/h

60o Triangle Books and Tools

B-21	14.95	Book - Sensational 6-Pointed Star Quilts	plus 2.00 s/h
B-10	14.95	Book - Building Block Quilts	plus 2.00 s/h
SR-20	16.95	Super 60 (Combination Triangle Tool)	plus 3.00 s/h
MP-3	11.50	8" Mini-Pro	plus 2.00 s/h
M-15	11.50	Metric Triangle	plus 2.00 s/h
CT-1	8.00	6" triangle	plus 2.00 s/h
CT-2	13.00	12" triangle	plus 2.00 s/h
GP-12	5.95	2-sided Graph Paper-Pad of 30 sheets	plus 2.00 s/h

Bargain Corner

SF – 8	5.00	Book - Stars and Flowers	plus 2.00 s/h
EA –7	5.00	Book - Easy & Elegant Quilts	plus 2.00 s/h
MA-14	5.00	Book - Mock Appliqué	plus 2.00 s/h
MC-16	4.00	Book - Merry Christmas	plus 2.00 s/h

For each additional item ordered subtract $1 from the shipping charges.
Wash. residents add 7.6% sales tax
We take Visa and Mastercard.
Tools usually shipped UPS
Books U.S. Mail

CLEARVIEW TRIANGLE
8311 - 180th St S. E.
Snohomish, WA 98296-4802 USA
Tel: 1-360-668-4151
Fax: 1-360-668-6338
Orders: 1-888-901-4151

E-mail: ClearviewT@cs.com
Web site:
http://ourworld.cs.com/ClearviewT

Special Thanks To These Manufacturers

Fairfield Processing Corp.
Cotton Batting-Soft Touch® by Fairfield

Kelsul, Inc.
Quilter's "Dream" Cotton™ Batting

Fasco/Fabric Sales Co., Inc.
McCloskey's Staples™ Fabric

Mission Valley Textiles
100% Cotton Yarn-dyed Woven Fabric

Hoffman California International Fabrics

P&B Textiles

Concord House Fabric Collections

Rose & Hubble Textiles

Omnigrid, Inc.
Omnigrid Rulers for Rotary Cutting
Omnimat®